AF577207

THE SOUL'S SWEET SIMPLE MUSIC

Elbert Sherrod

THE SOUL'S SWEET SIMPLE MUSIC
Elbert Sherrod

Published by:
First Assist Publications
P.O. Box 608
Woodland Hills, CA 91365

Phone/Fax: (818) 700-3412

Library of Congress Control Number: 2002112119
ISBN: 0-9724865-4-2

Printed in the United States of America
10 9 8 7 6 5 4 3 2 1

CONTENTS

PART I
The Music of Life Exudes From All Nodes...

PART II
Quiet Contemplation Yields Small Scrubs and Weeds...

PART III
Time, Mind and Love

PART IV
The Children Around Us …
… The Children We See

PART V
From Soul To Soul …

Part I

THE MUSIC OF LIFE EXUDES FROM ALL NODES ...

I Believe in Women

I believe in you, your power, your intellect
and what you have proven in my life.
I respect you above all men as God's greater
creation... more than an equal.

In my life you have displayed your motherhood,
your womanhood, your sisterhood
and your undying friendship,
which has made me who I am.

Among men I have found a father,
brothers and some friends.
But only in your kind
have I found the true essence of me.

In you lies the full object
of my earthly affections.
You make me think of Christ
and what He must be like.

Yes, I believe in the Power of Women,
the power to conquer men,
to raise the World's children,
to define love.

The power to open up your wings
and gather all of the World's children in;
to protect them from men.
To nurture them and to send them on their way
full of love and hope.
I believe in the power you have
over hearts and minds
and the healing touch you give.

Yes, I believe in Women, for in You,
God has revealed to me His undying, eternal love.

These Hands

These hands, though I've had them all of my
life,
they are amazing to me.
I find myself captivated by them.
When I recall the work they've seen… the joy, the
pain.
A perfect pair, they seem identical in every sense.

In my palms I read every job,
everything I've picked and everything I've carried.
Why aren't they tired?
I've taken good care of them, though they've been
bruised, once broken, battered, beaten and
burned.
Still they hang on in there doing what I demand
of them daily.

Through them a world of discovery has come to
me…
The softness of my mother's skin.
The feel of a beautiful woman.
The grip of a trusted friend.
The unforgettable feel of frostbite.
The heat of a winter's night stove fire.

They've drunk in the taste of rain water,
caressed persimmons, picked peaches,
popped may pops, pulled rabbits from boxes,
cleaned all sorts of things;
and watered by hand rows and rows of land,
and touched tender places like babies' faces and
fancy laces;
dug up ditches, and worms and peanuts and
potatoes (both sweet and Irish flavors);
they've patted and prodded, smacked and
comforted.

They've typed and wrote, soothed and smote,
caused wiggles and giggles and chimneys to
smoke.
They've prayed, waved, shaved, acted, and
sweated;
cracked, ashed, snatched, toted, clapped and
wrapped.
They've taught and fought, stirred and buried.

Someone great said that the mind is the measure
of one.
But in real life a man is really only what his hands
have done.

The Dark Shunned Mistress of Time

Look what you have become,
past scorned,
but now, now so rare and precious
to this world as to defy all
that flies in the face of success,
of enduring hope, lingering long,
made free.

Forged from deep running rivers
of fire,
of faith,
of hope so strong,
so immovable it set a mark,
a mark upon you, no one can erase.
The years of your trying
hewed deep channels in your granite face.
And hued you, rich, deep and dark over time.

You breather of fire,
You fermenter of dreams,
You the Dark Shunned Mistress of Time.
You have returned to claim
Your place, Your throne, Your children.

Sweet Mistress, Beautiful You;
History will not forsake You, this time.
Elusive Time has claimed a Bride,
and it is You,
You the Dark Shunned Mistress of Time.

Subsistance Allant Mon Frère

(Keep Going My Brother)

Keep going my brother. You are at the precipice
of winning.

How can you know how deep the river runs,
how long
the untraveled road, how near your goal?

By this, that you have not yet failed.

Press on until the light flickers, until the wick
is spent
and the runny candle wax sizzles at the
death throws
of the last drowning flame.

Sinking, going under in a sea of waxwork,
of what has energized you and supported you
for so long.
Residuals of life's works.

A hot melted sea of wax.

Though your life is spent,
It can not be measured in the length of the wick,
nor in the amount of melted wax,
but that you are a flame that helps light the World
for someone like me to see God.

O Son of Mine

O son of mine, I still can hear you softly
singing songs to me, though you never did …
I see you walking in groves of tender shoots,
with pomegranates and figs of pleasure ripened;
so ripe they burst and spew essence in the air,
imbibed by every pore, pleasurable food for the
soul.

O son of mine, I feel your touch, beckoning me,
who so long absent from this paradise prepared.
I spend these days, these weary days,
in toil and sweat, in infinite quest to see your face,
to embrace you, though I never did.

O son of mine, I still can see your face,
with deep regrets and sorrows breaking
against me every day … though I never did.
I feel the scars, I hear the sweet refrains
of your calling out to me … in supple fields of
turquoise green,
in oasis clear, where cisterns swell, where founts
abound;
and luscious dews and you await to refresh my
weary panting soul
… though you never did … though you never did.

Escape

I feel life's sharp staves pressing in on me.
Round about from every side.
How can I Escape, except with
what hope here, I have today?
What has lived inside me,
what has not been combed away.
What have I missed today?
What have I been set free of...
... some trouble distorted
... scandals averted
... plots foiled
... disaster thwarted
... schemes ruined
... gossip made false
... lies delivered
... ten new vices
and new sins besides.
Teeth, big and small
combing a making free,
a keeping of liberty,
an Escape for me.

Shrouded Cloak

Take off your dark shroud…
That cloak of darkness.
Which in times past made you,
your ebony beauty and your essence invisible.
Which tried to take away your dignity and your
persona.
Take off your dark shroud…
O you deep dark pearl with pure
perilous pools.

Take off your dark shroud…
That garment of mourning,
which from the beginning hid you,
your refined, masculine qualities and your intellect.
Which tries to make you base, repulsive and
unfeeling.
Take off your dark shroud…
O you great one of the ancient motherland,
magnificent and mighty.

Take off your dark shroud…
That shrouded cloak.
Which in time will rob you,
of your youth and drain your vitality.
Which will try to make you ashamed, hateful and
indifferent.
Take off your dark shroud…
O you little sparkling night water whose waves
wind to the ocean.

Good and Dead

When my soul is calm, I'll be good and dead.
Dead to the World.

To all that this world means and stands for.
Yes, good and dead to the World.

That is, dead to its viserating stings, to its pangs
and throws.
Yes, good and dead, to dying.

On the morning of my death,
those who pride themselves in being my enemies,

will have wasted a night of scheming;
hours of planning to defeat me.

They won't matter,
because I'll already be good and dead.

Those few who love me, will say a prayer,
a prayer for the good and dead brother.

The Face of Death

There is a Death that is seldom recognized...

I've looked into this Death's face and so have you.
But it is not the same death we know and hate.

But the death of what exists there inside, waiting for
you to give birth to it. Waiting to become some
different form other than pure stored thought;

Other than stagnant ideas, other than
un-assuredness,
into something you don't care who loves or hates.

The death of the creative you.
Brash, arrogant, in words and thoughts.
In truncated pieces of life experiences,
some bitter, some repressed, some psychotic, some
fresh.

This is the beautiful part of you,
which can die long before they throw clods of
Kentucky bluegrass and dirt on what used to be
your
face
or before you're served up well done in little pieces
to fishes in Lake Michigan.

The you who howled to be released,
the you of innumerability.
You who conquered a kingdom and walked away,
laying down your crown.

There, they heralded you as true king,
with no heir apparent, save this death,
an interloper, son of perdition.

You turned it over to him, when you gave up free
thought,
natural discourse of the soul,
captured in the repositories of the mind.

All the jars you smashed and broke in fits of passion
over the years,
But that's not what lost them,
why they're gone now.

They laid there, still, for many years;
waiting for their returning savior and a new birth.
When you visited them, your kingdom,
you stepped on them like broken pieces of glass.

But they were still happy to see you,
for they were still alive then.
They died that day when you
incensed out of your mind,
vowed never to return.

Then that Son swept them out, as clean and empty,
as the day you were sent.
Then they died, taking with them the glorious you,
the King, the Conqueror of worlds yet unseen.

Yes, I've looked this death in the face
and so have you.

Part II

QUIET CONTEMPLATION YIELDS SMALL SHRUBS AND WEEDS...

Draining

Life flows out of Him like a river.
Rippling then welling up with great waves
as torrents back up at the mouth of the opening.

Too much to flow out at once, too much to get
through such a small orifice
as one lifetime, one age, one era.

Though it is not ceaseless, it empties into a basin
which leads to a pool and the pool has a draining,
a draining into the world.

Its leading edge moves fast, on top it spirals.
The size of the outlet to the world causes delay,
open chaos, splendid waiting, orderly delay in a
whirlwind.

Causing those near to excel and those far away to
offer great delay.
The same order which causes the old to die faster
and the young more slowly;
which gives to those who have and takes from the
wanton.

Creating the timeless abyss of answers, of miracles,
of ages to come, of clearing,
of something more than we can ever know.

Peering out from within is an eye, one single eye.
Clear as crystal, bright and blazing.
Through the draining, through the spiraling,
looking at me, looking at you,
exposing all coming into its gaze.
Moving closer day by day.
Ever growing in its piercing,
never closing in its fierceness.

Very frightful, very grave, seeing through me with
    cutting blades.
Empty, black and hollow too, pulling me, pulling
    you.
Are we coming or are we going, passing through
    with no direction.

In and out of the very mind of God.

Sweet Flowing Truth

Truth is moisture.
Truth is thirst quenching.
Truth soothes and wets the soul, like a summer's
sudden rain over the parched cracked earth.

As all living things need water to survive;
the same is true of Truth, it is required for spiritual
life.
As all living things are made of some part water;
so truth equally pervades all things which are
made.

Truth does not flow uphill,
but flows down filling all who have need.
Truth only needs a little crack, a small sliver
to get through and flood all with light.

"Liberty" and "Justice" drift upon the Sea of Truth.
Her stormy waves drive them both to new heights.
Ice cold Truth is good for a summer's day;
filled with the heat of lies and sweltering
oppression.

Like hail and sleet, as truth passes slowly through
cold, resistant environments, it becomes hard and
may hurt, when it finally comes down.

Truth has no need to run and cry through the
streets;
but sits on the front porch and rocks away the day.
Truth is the eternal yell of the forming universe,
still heard today.

Truth rings and sounds in our ears and in our
conscience.
For truth is nothing less than the very voice of God.

Perdition's Path

The opportunity for change is here, the chance
to change,
to regain my former self, to grasp hold of a new,
rekindled faith.
To traverse what was previously known and
practiced by my
ancestors, by me and my progeny.

To regain surrendered ground, to stare down
perdition and build
precious treasures, to ascend to the Holy Mountain.
To that place
of no night, of eternal sun, of no tears and fears.

Or by failing prepare to descend to Sheol, a place I
never asked
to go; where fools rush in. A place fit for the
destruction of souls.
A place for those who spill innocent blood ... who
though warned,
harm little ones; who hide in lurks of darkness, who
feed on vice,
corruption, hate, indifference, and ill will; and who
prefer death to all
power antecedents ...

Who took in one full breath of life and spewed it
out, preferring to
imbibe the bitter wormwood of death ... Who
chose weeping to joy,
sorrow to rejoicing, this life to eternity; to hurt men
instead of seeking
wisdom; to rather hate self, than love any other ...

Who seek the utopia of Hell by the deluding drug
of present pleasures ...

Who only need a few misguided souls for
accompaniment on the journey …
Who teach avarice and apathy; and prefer trapping
of fools to other evil men …
Who encase souls, caged, bound early in life and
bound for Perdition.

Senseless youth, the hateful aged, the unaware, the
thrill-seeker, the learned,
the lame, the whole, the rich, the poor, the
religious, heads of states.

All outnumbered on Perdition's Path, by the spent,
wasted and used Fool.
And why for such a "paltry bag of beans" as the
"here and now,"
would you sell your soul to Hell?

Why indeed, for Hell is denied, for the fool has
really said that there
is no Hell. While the wise contemplate the matter.

Who could blame these poor misguided souls …
Who must die to
discover the weight of their error; the depth of their
depravity …
Who say "such a place as Hell would stink to High
Heaven, thereby
warning all of its presence."
Awake you Fool and imbibe the smell of Hell.
Starting with me,
the hurt I've caused, the fear engendered.

My life, full of my own bitterness biting, pulling,
tugging at me.
Miserizing my life, clinging, sticking, pressing,
keeping me from blessings.
Choking out with weeds of sorrow and discontent,
my life, old, frustrated and spent.

If ever a life was fit for destruction and nature
and all creation groans to eat me up.
To send me back to the Pit where all fireballs
derived.

It is near the end of my life.
I smell something burning!
Burning flesh?
Is it Hell?
No, but a sweet savor to God,
a sacrifice taking my sins and your sins away.

Give it All to Christ

God is anyone's life more black?

We live between the slivers of the Blackness.
That is where life really is.
A cone of darkness, event upon event
of unmitigated failure, surrender, thought and
emotion.

Seething, writhing, ebbing, flowing,
ceaseless, draining, dark and unholy.
Waiting for a Savior;
waiting for the reality of deliverance.

For one real thing;
one event which tells us there's hope.
One sliver of light to light the faces of the ones we
call love
or to light the acts we thought were good and holy.

Has it come?
Have we seen it?

All turns and fades to black again with rest.
And quiet contemplation yields only "small shrubs
and weeds";
when we desire and need the holiness of
"Tall Oaks and Cedars."
Will the darkness fade, or should we live in its
shroud?

We do.
Do we care?

No, for a million of our dreams have vanished into
the night.
Taking with them what could be real to us.
And then the day breaks in on our reality;
arousing fools, who still slumber, yet awake.

Destitute of any remaining feelings of pain.
It's crazy, still and calm be over.

Reality contemplated is dark, O so very dark.

Christ, help me to turn the darkness into light.
Save me from what I see each day; from what I live
each day.
From my past, from my present,
from what should be my future.

Save Lord and then relieve;
in You the darkness doth subside.
In Your name the soul has slowly learned to trust,
to take our solace in.

A Name to calm, to shadow the dark,
the blackness, bringing light.

A hope against hope, a resting-place,
sanity among chaos, sweetness that is real.

The Observer's Praise

I observe the mountain before me,
in all its majesty.

Awed by it, shall I bow down to it,
for it is mother of my flesh?

She made me and bore me,
from her deep earthly womb.

I observe the sea around me,
in all its magnificence.

In all its splendor, shall I worship it
for it is truly the father of my flesh?

He endowed me with all that is me,
from his infinite treasures of the deep.

I observe the wind and tide
and all the elements.

Hypnotized by their motion, shall I imbibe them,
for they are the life of my soul to me?

They fill me all in all
and give me space and substance.

I observe the full creation
in its chaotic order.

Charmed by its cycles and sequences,
shall I sing praises to the creation?

For it is my spirit, it
moves me on my course through life.

I observe time and history,
in recorded splendor.

Fascinated by them, shall I hallow them,
for they are my life?

They teach me wisdom
and give me a sense of eternity.

I observe the universe through the starry night
sky, in its cloak of darkness.

Enraptured by it, shall I yield up to it my body,
my soul, my spirit, my life?

Then I knew the answer, affirmed by the starry
night sky, that I shall praise my God,
the Creator of all things.

For He alone is worthy of the Observer's
adoration, worship, and praise...

And all Observers of the creation shall sing praises
to Him in the Final and Great Assembly.

I Can Not Know You

God, You are like nothing else there is.

As my mind tries to grasp some expressible likeness
of Your attributes, Your character; You escape my
senses my ability to grasp You, to know You.

I employ all that You have endowed in me, in my
body, in my soul, to obtain one "true" likeness of
You, Your power, Your grace, Your mercy, Your
love.
O to fully know "one thing" that is truly You…
Yours alone… would be divine.

You wonderfully and fearfully made my body,
but through it, I can not know You.
You endowed me with all my natural senses,
but through them, I can not know You.

I see Your lighting trail through the sky,
I hear Your rolling thunder.
I feel Your heavenly dew drops drench my body.
I taste Your sweet truth running down my face and
I smell the refreshing newness You bring.
All in one summer rain, yet I can not know You.

One grassy plain, though teeming with life,
only lightly whispers Your name.
I hear the strong lion roar and I wonder.
I see endless herds of living things...All like me,
wandering and unable to know You, to see You.

I feel Your sun over my skin, giving me life.
Do You hear my soul thanking You?
As I stand and gaze.
I taste salty tears, rolling down,
for I can not know You.

I have felt you in those images
brought to me from the depths of Your sea.
Things no other generation has seen or known.

I see You when the depths are lit and
Your wonders move about.
I hear You in the knowledge that though the depths
may crush me to powder;
Your marvelous creatures thrive and bask there.

I hear You in a ring, an eternal ring,
coming down from the beginning of things.
When Adoil pregnant with the Universe,
with all things, erupted.

It tunes my heart and I have my being.
Yes, I always hear it…
but it brings me no news of You.
O, I have seen the images
from the outreaches of Your space.

Ever probing deeper and deeper
into Your infinite creation.
Images of nebulous worlds spiraling through space,
hurled so far with such force
as to appear in eternal motion.

And I know that most of what "Is" can not be seen,
as "You" can not be seen.
Why are You the Invisible God?
Why are Your ways higher than our ways?
Why can't our senses bring us to You?

I have heard that You are a "Spirit" and must be
obtained and worshiped in the "Spirit."
God, one last question. What is a "Spirit"?

I can not know You…

Dichotomy of Soul

Caught in this body is a dichotomy of soul.
One the freeborn child of a King, the returned
prodigal, the heir of promises.

The other a compacted, self-contained core
of darkness, evil, blight and endless lust.

All in one, all in me.
It's time to blossom to expand to delight.

Though in you dwells nothing pure, nothing
wholesome, nothing sweet or demure.

The Universe

Are You alive or are You chance and
circumstance?
We observe only one scale of Your beauty
and nigh faint from awe.
Are we of You by condition of God?

You rage, but we are still.
You wander, but we are at rest.
You are as it seems infinite
and we are so very finite.

Your diamonds light up the night sky.
Your fiery rubies burn through the brightest day.
Your deep dark coldness, stills life.
Your cold dark matter is invisible.
Your Dark Angels, capture, plunder and spew out
galaxies.
Your children are billions upon billions of worlds,
all different.

To the unaware you appear as God.
To the aware as God's cloak.
You are a glorious work indeed.
Are You the very mind of God Himself?

Apocalypse

Divinely hallowed caverns
unknown to men,
storing "Pharaoh's Curse"
in the end.

Somewhere two rivers meet,
fire and ice, water and gold;
is forming in translucent sheets,
slabs for streets.

Yes, he can, but one dip from his finger
made the gulf wormwood;
vengeance of bitter gall,
so he declined to drink at all.

No one knew but years before a dark angel
swallowed a tri-fold inverse of stars.
The Heavens quote the Devine, with the delayed
diligence of the dark angel's devastation

The cosmological constant halts, stillness,
the forming ring of the universe
replaced with a scream,
"the tares, the tares, only the tares"

A command … "stay the hands of the dark ones,
which boil the elements in blood,
now release, release … for creation screams,
in pangs of birth … in newness screams,
'It is done.'"

And upward goes the Heaven's scroll,
and downward to earth the Savior goes.
The Judgment Seat of God to share.
The end, the end of evil men.

Part III

TIME, MIND AND LOVE...

Esprit mis en Bouteille (Bottled Essence)

A voice as the fragrance of juniper,
squeezed with an esthetic twist.

Strained by thinly veiled promises,
whispers of what is commonly known,
can never be.

Platitudes offered, hanging like
thousand year stalactites
in freshly hewn caves, surreal.

Something more befitting dust and damnation,
than hallowed delirium
and desired years of jubilation.

Reverberating at mach,
uttering, echoing provocation which ought only be
thought and then dismissed.

Sorrows stored in alabaster boxes with serenades,
canned and wrapped waiting for delivery.

Anticipation starting to rise as lurid sky high
fireworks,
and finishing as effervescence bursting
just above the nose.

Dispersing light mist and any real hope, yet
clouding the mind with thoughts of quiet suffering
and years of expectation.

Dreams

Dreams are our soul's adventures, our trembling,
frightful quests into the unknown corridors of our
minds.

It takes a crisis to bring us back from our soul's
aimless wanderings.
But after each crisis a little less of us comes back
each time.

Until finally, in our soulful adventures
we stammer and fall;
faltering and faint,
we finally don't come back at all.

We fear ourselves more than any foe imaginable;
we quake at the guarded unexplored fringes
and forbidden places of our minds.

While we sleep we stab aimlessly at the dark,
that if by chance a foe is near,
that unacquiescent spirit that we fear.

We'll stab and pierce and cut it under, and when
the churning turmoil of the night is through
and the twilight of our dreams has ended.
Then looking by the morning light.
We see something bludgeoned in the night.

As we draw closer to the fallen foe.
We see and know;
we fight only against ourselves in every dream.

Time, Mind and Love

It's time for heart and mind
and soul to unite;
for dreams and wishes
and conjured emotions to take flight.

It's time for the birth
of a new, vibrant and real thing;
for the decline of an old,
dreary but rare thing.

It's time to make a stand or—
to fall;
to live,
to chance,
to tell all.

To empty the mind—
of its secret passions,
of its particular fashions,
of its sickening modes,
of its plots in groves.

To end its corruption—
its ceaseless sombers,
its wakenings;
its drifting through tranquil seas,
its gentle settings;
its pleasant plottings,
its woeful passions,
its incessant pleadings,

its churnings,
its bleedings,
… to release me.

New worlds are made with three simple letters,
Y-E-S.
And still greater ones with two, N-O.
Yet to the "Mind" no preference to either given,
Its course decided it will deliver.

No, "Time" waits for no man,
for it is present at every moment.

Yet "Mind" is space and real and fabric.
Still "Heart," not "Mind" but "Love" is greatest.

SHE

So it is She, the one I love,
a streak of darkness in the night.

Marauding bands of time have not carried away her
goodness.
My desire still rages incessantly.

She is captivating, no less than any army, only one,
but strong.
In her grip there is no swaying, no relief, no fall.

'Tis true, no weapon formed against love can stand.
All traps laid are laid to waste.

She exudes all that is natural, all that is me,
even as she sleeps.

She is a work of grand design.
As if carved from a dream long forgotten.

Packaged and wrapped in disguise,
still yet indistinguishable from what was seen.

All designed with my heart in mind.
She is one of a kind.

Everyday

Everyday you're away,
seems to make me stronger.
Everyday without you,
makes me want you no longer.

Every passing hour of my suffering,
makes me resist you.
Every counted empty minute,
makes me less and less miss you.

Every night that escapes to morning.
Every passion I keep from forming.
Moves me from joy to mourning,
and more along the road of getting over you.

Every night in the still and passionless evening,
when your vision comes a'teasing.
I can resist you with thoughts displeasing,
and calm my rapid breathing.

Every unfulfilled night with tossing and turning,
with passion's fuel a'burning.
With frantic restless churning,
moves me closer to my learning of getting over you.

Every empty moment that I can stand,
moves me closer and closer to a plan.
That helps me extricate the vision
and the loneliness brought by you.

Every thought now again I'm controlling;
while my soul I'm now consoling.
Of the thing from it thought stolen,
yet it still will go a'strolling, on peaceful shores
without you.
Every week spent in this condition,
seems to improve my gloomy disposition.

And moves me on without remission,
to the sunny shores of admission,
that I can make it without you.

Every month of my new healing,
brings me glorious thoughts and feelings.
And gratitude in suffering revealing,
that though now my mind is still reeling,
I can make it without you.

Every new year of my contemplation,
brings me wondrous revelations.
Of how with sheer will and determination,
though through pain and consternation,
I made it without you.

Though my body's still rebelling,
and my heart rate is still excelling.
Though the fires are still a'flaming,
and my soul is still complaining.

When my clock starts alarming,
and the night turns into morning.
And the maddening passions of the night's
restless churning, fade into the dizzying dew
of my morning running.

Then I know, I made it "one more night"
without you.

Some Life

Go now and quickly liven up my dreams.
Be sure to return, just before my day begins.
I'll certainly need you in it to get through.
I've learned to depend on you for such things
as day brightening and reasons for living.

While you're busy living that wonderful
life you have,
drop a few crumbs for me to get by on.
Oh didn't you know that the dogs feed on what's
dropped from the master's table.
A veritable feast in pieces of someone else's life.

You've lived a good life.
Why not spend a few moments of your valuable
time
to cheer the fallen, to help some wayward
soul like me.
Who never learned the joyous side of life.
I'll do all I can to show my appreciation.

It's just that I'm a pauper at life, a failure at living,
at loving, at paying homage to the glorious
celebration of it all.

And you, you exude life,
so gifted in the issuance of life.

You Are a Poem to Me

You are a Poem to me.
Your pentameters are amazing to see.
May your rhythm and your rhyme,
last, til the end of all time.
While I thirst,
after your every verse.

Yes you are a Poem to me,
as anyone who reads you will agree.
There's heartbreak and pain,
in your every refrain, and soul stirring misery.
But there's also tenderness, which comes from
above, in your epic story of love.

Yes, you are a Poem my dear
and Poets everywhere have somewhat to fear.
For you're not written by the hands of men,
but you're directly from God's Holy Pen.
Now, since you are God's Poem written to me,
I'll commit you to my memory.

I'll learn all of your lines, your rhythm and rhymes
and discover in you, all that God meant me to see.

I Wish the Day

Such days as these I wish I had not seen.
If only I could press the rising sun back to its rest.
But I know each day the brilliant sun will rise
and with it bring teary eyes.
Such hurt must come,
with healing as close as a wagon hitch away.

These days come now too quickly for me.
With no time to agonize over the events of
yesterday,
or to promptly begin my worries for tomorrow.
All is undone, I'm losing time,
it's spilling all over the place.

What a waste.

Perfectly good hours spent on end,
at tasks with no redeeming value.
Nothing of any lasting goodness,
nothing which helps plug this hole
of endless draining time.

What a waste.

I don't care too much for sleep tonight,
though, I suspect I'll need it in the morning.
The issues of life have caught me fast and heavy
and won't let me move on to greater things.

What a dreadful waste…

Yesterday and Today

Yesterday I was happy, today I am sad.
Yesterday I could sleep,
but today I just toss and turn.
Yesterday I had focus and clarity of mind.
Today there's confusion with never enough time.

Yesterday I contemplated the glories of GOD.
Today I scribble the words of a fool.
From joy to pain all in one moment dissolved
But inside my mind several years have evolved.

Yesterday I was me, today I am new.
Yesterday I was calm, rational and sane.
Today these qualities, I try to regain.

Yesterday I was at,
a certain place that was safe.
Today I am bewildered
by the troubles I face.

Since yesterday I have changed.
Today I can never be the same.

I see everything
from a new point of view.
But my goal today,
will be to undo the new.

Yesterday I liked
and controlled all my thoughts.
Today my brain is at rest
and I think from the heart.

I will negotiate with today,
to release what it caught,
While I try to relearn,
the things I was taught.

Today is today
and today is just fine.
But I am yesterday
and yesterday will again be mine.

Opposed

You are a mystery beyond figuring out.
And I stopped trying, but I can't stop caring,
or turn off your meaning something to me.

Your soul seems to be asking for something that
I'm not giving,
or that's even in me to deliver.
I keep trying and failing,
you call it lying and rebelling.

I agree with all the blackness you see in me,
but when you look at me, you have to see you *in*
me. When and if you do, can you apply the
forgiveness you give to yourself to me?

The forgiveness that you use to present yourself to
me
as something rare and wonderful,
and as someone infinitely worth the change your
soul is requesting of me.
The same forgiveness that allows your soul to
accept whatever goodness you find in me,
as something you deserve and have been
waiting for.

Why does your soul reject all that I stand for,
all that I am?
As if for your survival, you must see me fallen,
crushed and broken.

I'm sorry that I represent all other hurtful people to
you.
All the pain and suffering you've been through, all
the hurt.
I'm sorry that I have an ego,
like other hurtful people in your life,
I'm sorry that when I use the word "I"
that your soul says, "It's all about selfishness."

I'm sorry that life hurt you, and that,
I can't cure you of those hurts.
I'm sorry that you thought that I could.

I too am blind and can't lead the way back home.
The way back to innocence,
The way back to the little child,
Who believed in life and love and the wonderful
difference between a man and a woman,
between a father and a mother.

I too am lost forever.
I too have been hurt by mother, man, father and
woman.
I don't know the way.
I only know that it's getting darker and darker
and I'm lost too, and can't get home.

If we touch hands in the darkness,
we can hold on or let go and face it alone.
Or we can fight each other in the darkness,
as if we have found the true enemy of our soul,
the true root of our pain.

I know there is good in you in your soul,
I see it and accept it.
I know of the other things that lie there
and accept those as part of you.

I'm asking you to accept the good in me and also
know that there are other things
also, baggage, which comes with life,
with trying and living.

3:30 AM

Anxiety visits me every morning at around 3:30.
That old friend.
Some call the blues.
Lying with me in my bed.
Keeping me awake at night.
Who said, "good morning heartaches" …
… I know what you mean.

Part IV

THE CHILDREN AROUND US…

…THE CHILDREN WE SEE

The Children

The children around me,
the children I see,
I feel their power, I share . . . I care.
I see their brilliance,
their feelings, bewildered,
their names embolden
and staggered they fight.

The children of suffering,
The children of trial.
These wonderful children,
The children we love.
How will we help them?
How can we care for what has been
placed in our charge?

We have not always done right by them.
Keep them, hold them, build them, mold them.
They are somewhat different from us.
We see God in their eyes,
They will overcome all
and ascend to the Holy Mountain.
God will save the children.

Little Girl

Little Girl, you amaze me
as you grow before my eyes.
You never stop learning
and needing and wanting.

God blessed you
and has given you so much.
He has truly
and richly smiled upon you.

Live your life,
joyfully, peaceful and free.
Without fear, with love and with the eyes
of your understanding opened wide.

You are already more than I could imagine.
You are more than my hopes and prayers
when I prayed for you.

Little Girl, you mean the world to me.
Little Girl, I love You.

Running Little Sparkling Night Water

All of my life you've been running away from me.
I lost you once for a few minutes in a department store.
Then you ran all the way to school.
You ran to summer camp.
You ran to your room, where you took refuge.
You ran to a distant place in your mind,
where no one could get to,
where even I couldn't find you to bring you back.

Somewhere at the right rear of your brain,
somewhere, abstract fields of honeysuckle roll,
through hills of lilac and entrenched dreams.
A place were girls and boys frolic,
with no thoughts of tears
or sequenced thoughts of shame or disgrace.

Somewhere your mind grew wings,
with which you flew to places previously only
dreamed.
Beyond the small boundary, the horizon of
consciousness.
Beyond belief and beyond what others wanted for
you.
You flew to where You, Yourself were waiting with
a cup of tea and a smile that said "now, I'm free."
"I am a Free Thinker, a Lover of Dreams ...
a Keeper of Destiny ...
I am Me, "Running Little Sparkling Night Water"
flowing out to Shining Big Sea Water,
running out to life."

The Dancing Girl

She danced so beautifully when first
I saw her.
She danced right into my heart.
Oh how she danced and danced and danced.
Up one side of the mountain and down the other.

Her eyes never opened, not for a moment.
Her mind never swayed from her blissful
  sequence.
Twirling and spinning and spinning and twirling.
Oh dainty flower of the dew of dawn.
The dancing girl danced on and on.
Pricking and prancing, wild, unconsciously free.

"Salutations," I cried, "Salutations," she replied.
Then the dancing girl opened her eyes.
Her greeting was like the blissful rain
that falls upon the desert plain.
A cautious word, a gentle smile,
and from her eyes the rainbow rise.

A soulful turn a graceful glance,
and off she goes again to dance
And in her kind demure way,
she beckoned me to seize the day.

"Why do you dance so fancy and free,
  without a care?"
She said, "Dancing's my bliss, my passion, my love.
Dancing's my gift from above."

"And why is it ceaseless,
  with never an end?"
"I dance 'til the music within me subsides."
"I've heard no music, no rhythm," I replied.
Quietly still standing on pirouetted toes,
She said, "The music of life exudes from all nodes.

It's in the flowers, the basins of rain;
the ecstasies of life, the sorrows the pains.
The music's in me and in you as well.
When I hear it, I dance as the cisterns swell.
The soul's sweet simple music,
        that exudes from all nodes."

"How can I hear it, how can I dance?
How can I twirl and mimic and prance?
How did you first hear it?
Can you show me the way?"

"Quietly sitting under God's creation one day.
Quietly sitting alone just with me.
Quietly sitting under a tree.
In just that moment, my soul started to sway.
My soul took flight, my spirit unbound.
With that my body started twirling around.
I have not ceased to dance,
since that soul stirring day."

"Salutations," I said, "Salutations," said she.
"I'm off," I said, "to find that tree."
A pitiful look she gave me with a glide.
"It's not in the tree, it's all from inside."

Then with a twist she circled me round, and
beckoned something from inside me deep down.
Something left me that day, I didn't know what at
        the time.
But now I know she extracted that soul's sweet
        simple music of mine.
To use in her dancing.
What she knew I'd never find.
Then she twirled and spun out of view…
and now here I sit under a tree,
while the Dancing Girl dances,
        on and on, with my soul through eternity.

I Tried to Hide

Once I tried to hide from God,
where to hide I did not know.
Where from God could I go?

First I thought underneath a pinecone seed,
a fitting place to hide indeed.

But there underneath the tiny pinecone seed;
God sent a flea to trouble me.

Then I hid in a small root of a weed;
underneath the earth where I couldn't be seen.

Still God found me in the root of the weed
and caused an aphid to make me flee.

"Now I see," I said,
"I must hide in the deep, deep sea instead."

God even found me in the deep, deep sea
and sent a dolphin to rescue me.

Then I tried something out far,
I hid myself in a Quasar.

Then God said, "despite the brightness of that star,
I still know exactly where you are."

Then I tried to hide inside a man's eye;
but God simply gave tears to make him cry.

Once I tried to hide from God,
where to hide I did not know.
Where from God could I go?

So never again from Him will I hide,
But ever under His mighty wings abide.

In Earth, in Sky, in Space, in Time;
God always finds this face of mine.

And presses it with His gentle hands
and beckons me to Buellah Land.

Are You There?

God do You mind if we fly,
up in the sky?
Do You still care,
when we're up there?

Are You angry with those who go
down under the sea?
Do You still see them
like You see me?

God do You care if men venture thus to climb,
the highest peak,
the highest place that they can find?

Will You still calm their frights,
while they're way up there at night?

And is the entire human race,
accursed for going out in space?

Will You be there with Your cross,
when he lands on Andromeda?

Are You angry when we sin
and let the evil Satan in?

Will Thou withstand us with our foe?
Wake us, will Thou when we have woe?

All Caught Up on Goodbyes

I'm all caught up on goodbyes.
In case the night takes me by surprise.

I remember when sleeping and waking belonged to
me,
or so I thought from what I could see.

One day I awoke and realized
that waking was a gift from God.
And sleeping more precious still.

Now-a-days I try to live in the moment.
Never assuming even the next second is promised
me.

Though health and strength are now my constant
companions,
still no more than one breath each moment I take.

Drawing one in and pushing it out.
One breath short of all life's fears and doubts.

One breath away from Heaven's Gate.
One breath away from "my soul to take."

Didn't I already say goodbye to you?
I live goodbye in all I do.

I Shall Smile Again

I shall smile again, but not like before. My laughter
and frolic will be as if on sorrow's
shipwrecked shore.

I shall smile again though through clenched teeth.
With sighs and always with inward reflection,
with pain mixed laughter in grief.

I shall smile again no matter how miserable this
world can be.
No matter how inconsiderate to smile again feels to
me,
I'll smile, you'll see.

I shall smile again though my heart is weak and
trembling.
I shall smile again despite the dark clouds
assembling.

Life will make us smile or we slowly die,
of sorrows too dismal, too unholy, to deny.

Yes if we live, we smile,
if only for a little while.

Following

We were not sure which way to go.
We were lost and saw a cracked door.
We peeked through and they pulled us in.
At least there is some light here.
Where we were before was very dark.
No one told us what the purpose was after we
came in.
A group of us came in together.
We started taking directions and doing some of
what we were told.
Those that did more, left the rest of us behind.
A few went back through the cracked door,
we had entered.
More might have gone back also,
but they showed us other doors, in other places,
that were better for opening and going through.
They all had light.
None had the darkness, the emptiness we
remembered.
They scolded us and told us to try to forget the
darkness.
Some of us did forget, those who did left us behind.
The rest of us, the slow ones,
spent most of our times in rooms behind the many
doors.
They were always filled with some of us, who came
in together.
They taught us how to leave like the others, who left
us behind.
They told us not to think about them and some
didn't.
Those who didn't, left us behind.
Then one day we looked around
and the room was empty except for one of us who
came in.
We didn't know what to do.
Everyone who entered the door with us, was gone.

They left us behind. Then they told us that we
had to learn to leave or we would stay in rooms
    forever.
The fear of being alone made us learn to leave.
Finally the last of us who had come in together left.
Then they told me what my purpose was.

Moonshine

I never met him but My Gran Pappy
was always talking bout that
Ol' trickster Moonshine, how he steal away
every night looking for mischief for some wheres
to lay his Ol head, for some'em to make bright.

He stay wake, long into the morning.
Just a'shining and a'grinning and pretending,
that he some em, even trying to outshine the sun.

Yep, my Ol Cajun Gran Pappy say, Moonshine
always be happy ...
Cause his belly always half full or full with crescent
o' gratin ...
And he ain't never have to pick no cotton ...
And he gots a servant man just sitting there
watching.

Gran Pappy, He say, Moonshine even gots
some spirits named after him.
Moonshine go round striking folk
and driving 'em crazy.
Still everybody he touch
fall in love with Moonshine.

Yep, that Ol Moonshine was some kinda trickster.

A Runner A Racer

Set a goal.
Run with the goal within your sight.

Keep your eyes focused on the goal.
With each step it comes closer into focus.
The goal is pulling you to it. It's fast, it's real time.
You reach your goal quickly and almost without effort.

You discover the race is not over.
That goal was one of many needed to complete the race.
You are not pleased by the discovery but even more determined.
You continue with a new goal, keeping the pace.

You're halfway there and picking up momentum.
You feel good, strong and smart.
You turn for the final stretch,
Your body responds, you're almost there.

You feel the surge, it mounts, you respond, you're there.
It's over, you realize that you had no foe other than yourself.
You compete against yourself in every race.
And you realize that this was "one run," "one race."
Then all comes into focus;
as a Runner you have many races, many goals.
Everything in life is a race and you never stop running.
You never stop setting goals, you never stop finishing.

You are "a Runner, a Racer."

Part V

FROM SOUL...
...TO SOUL

History

Arise, Arise, Old Slumbering Scribe,
Old Ancient Scribbler, Old full of eyes.
Awake, Awake, and cross the waters,
for another who sleepeth has been revived.

Go now go quickly and begin,
for one so worthy of thy pen,
has stirred, gathered Herself,
and walks this mighty way again.

Awake I say, Awake,
for Noble History's sake.
Awake and cross the sea.
Swim Old Great One, toward the western bend,
toward the Free.

Come see, Come see, thine heir apparent,
full of splendor, pomp and grandeur.
Whilst thou tarries, she has enslaved
and freed and enslaved again,
whilst thou meanders.

She has blown the trump of war,
and carried the torch of hypocrisy.
She roared, conquered, and stretched
out her borders from sea-to-sea.

And will thou record her in thy favor,
a Rebel, Libertine, Zealot or Savior?
And of Her great works from shore-to-shore,
will they last forever more?

Speaketh thou of her great devices,
of which the world will never tire?
That squeaked and roared and zoomed and glided,
that set this mortal world afire.

Awake, I say, but still He sleeps,
not a stir, not a peek.
As if to say, "I will not rise,
I have already recorded all Lies."

"In other times, in other places,
with other rhetoric, through different faces."
"In days of yore, in times of old,
I'm sorry but Her story's told."

"I rise no more for futile nations,
but sleepeth on through selfish, cursed
generations."
"Til Last, I rise to complete the work,
that chronicles mankind's self inflicted hurts."

"Then and only then, I rise, to open up the
Judgement Book, into which only One dare look."

"Then She, as all the rest may see,
that there is only "pain" in Human History."

Fallen Soldiers
(The Marching Dead Full of Dread)

They marched from here to Inchon Way,
toiled, embattled, the meek, the enslaved,
the doomed ones.

Pressing on to oblivious heights they marched,
with fear their soul mate and their guide.
Searching out the unsearchable, the marching dead
full of dread, searching out their resting place.

With signs of irrevocable blankness on their faces,
they marched on to their appointed hour.
Thousands to their left and thousands to their
right,
but singled out for untold acclaim.

Knew they of their impending demise,
written in their fellows' eyes, while marching on?
They lived and breathed and ate and died
as all the living do.

They laughed and cried aloud,
but not in their hour, their purpose set,
their souls delayed,
their lives laid bare for all to see.
Commanded for strife, demanded to fight,
mustered up all hopes and fears
and memories that courage requires.

Timeless are their marching boots,
wordless were their final salutes.
The marching dead, full of dread,
marching on to their close.

132nd Street Jack Sprat

That Lady staying with Jack,
she don't eat nothing but fat.

And you know Jack don't do
nothing but drink Jim Beam.
That's why between them both you see,
They're sharing an ICU room
up at Martin Luther King.

From Soul to Soul

So speaks one soul to another.
Something which starts as a feeling without voice,
on its upward journey.

Given substance by the body's aches and pains
and deeply hewn emotions.
Something which picks up strength from sinew
and depth from strength of heart.

Something the mind randomly labels,
finding some ascribable cause and effect.
Some reason for every groaning of the soul.
So as to keep things moving upward,
flowing upward.

Towards the hard rocky white peaks
or what remains of them.
Over the tumultuous untamable red sea
and through the great divide.

Then something incredibly remarkable happens,
...the meeting of two souls.

For that first something without voice is now
something resonating in open space, real, deep,
propagating at mach and aimed at another soul.

It pierces through flesh, bone and marrow.
This once silent feeling, with no expression,
no discernment, no guilt, no sin.

Will it now kill and destroy or resurrect?
No matter which, for another great mind, strips
away causes, ascribed emotions, heart and sinew.

Washing and bleaching until it is ready for the soul.
Something sweet, simple and understandable
    between souls,
with life and misunderstanding taken out.

A sigh, where I feel your pain
or a jovial laugh and I feel your joy.

Modern Chronicles

Novelists endeavor to parchments supreme,
never stopping to examine even the slightest dream.
Composing tea leaf chronicles that tell lies,
unadulterated lies,
with twisted plots...spiraling, corkscrewing with deep
roots down into Sheol.

Cotton Mouth Incident on the Pamlico

Remember the summers we'd fish on the creek at
Crawford's Landing?
How you would do anything to go fishing?

"The fishing won't be any good," Ma'd say;
"it looks like quick rain,"
And how we begged until she recanted?
We marched like triumphant soldiers three abreast,
poles on shoulders, barefoot down the hot, dusty,
dirt road, with squishing hot sand between our
gritty toes.

Down and past the gate at Bonus Acres,
through the big horse meadow, full of big black
        bumble bees,
        armor piercing June bugs and stink weeds.
We'd run the gauntlet of sand spurs, cockleburs,
biting yellow flies, with morning glory vines
wrapping around our ankles and toes.

Remember the smell of quick rain in the air?
The kind that barely wets the hot dust,
the kind that hardly gets your feet wet.

Remember how the bay opening so suddenly, would
take us by surprise;
and the smell of goggle eye, mullet and
        perch in the air?
Remember the refreshing taste and
feel of the open bay in the cool of the evening?
Native Americans called it "Chocowanateth..."
"Fish from many waters."
We called it our "Heaven" our "Home."

Ma was right again when it finally came;
we never caught fish in the rain.
Remember when I got bored, and laid down my
pole
to investigate a leaping, croaking
bullfrog
in the shallows near the tall reeds?
And how I slowly reached down between the thick
reeds
and gripped it by the spine so as not to get warts?

How I turned to you and lifted high my prize;
noting the surprise in your silver dollar-size eyes,
I thought what a gigantic
catch I must have made.

How I turned to see what was in my own hands
and threw the six-foot water moccasin
attached to the frog's leg,
ten feet into the air and
moved like lightening, shouting, O Jersey!

Remember how you both laughed,
at my fright all the way back
through the big horse meadow,
through the gauntlet, the gate at Bonus Acres
and back to Ma and civilization, alive…

...Dreaming of uncaught fish,
bullfrogs and water moccasins all night long.

Time's Illusion

Time is a wonderful illusion
given man to make his day.
Most of the sensible ones have learned by now
that time does not exist.

There is only a spinning and a chasing.
No night, only a shadow,
a trick with cosmic dust and lights.

No years or seasons
only revolving and spinning,
an illusion from the beginning.

The moon has no light of her own to give.
She has bewitched you, a trick with mirrors.

Mother Earth is enslaved by that tyrant the Sun.
What reason for this slavery what has she done?

She captured Sister Moon and wouldn't let her go.
Sister Moon will get her day in solar court,
you know.

Mother Earth sent a delegation to flag Sister Moon.
Sister Moon is still crying from the hurt
she assumed.

Freeway Poet

Who are all of these people
and why are they going where I'm going?

Don't they know that I like to travel alone?

Did they ever stop to think
that I might need privacy, space?

How inconsiderate of them all
to follow me as they do.

Some even have the nerve to pass me.

God, you must be something special
to have made all of these people.

Simon's Bad Rap

"Are you Simple Simon,
who met a pieman going to the fair?"

"Yea, I'm Simon.
And what business is it of yours if I buy a 100 pies,
from that brother that always wears them bow ties?

"No, I ain't going to no damn fair!
I'm going over 52nd street
and ain't no fair over there!

"Naw, are you crazy, you ain't see 'me'
        on no corner,
asking someone to taste 'somewhere'!

"Naw, are you 'the man'?

"Nobody asked me for no penny.
It was a dime bag and I still didn't buy any.

"Yea, I told you, I'm Simon!
But somebody lying on me,
I ain't *said* or *did* nothing."

Southern Nights

They sizzle.
They fry.
Cool breeze through the willows, occasionally.
Children running wild, bare feet.
A wiener roast.
Boys tongue tied, with nothing meaningful to say.
Gasping for something.
Fast girls with quick minds,
giggle at, laughing at and scorning slow boys.

Mosquito bites, yellow lights.
Rainy nights.
Southern nights.

The smell of freshness in the air.
Running barefoot through puddles.

Voluptuous women and laughing, grinning men,
dancing to the jukebox tunes.

Southern nights.
The music's right,
to dance all night.

Southern nights.
Saturday night.
Waterfront site.
Take my Baby to Club Elite.
Those Steamy Southern Nights.

Carry Home

When that day comes,
what will be our end?
What will they say about us?
How we lived or how we died?
Our living must not be in vain.
All flesh must go, the question is when and how.
All in due time, but never timely.
We fill our days with these morbid
contemplations overwhelming our senses,
piling up dissensions and fears.
Then comes the night with its ruminations on
actions taken in the day.
May we not carry this life
in fear of commoners or kings;
and may the dirty eyes close all around us.
For if it were not for those truths we live by,
at the end we would not carry home.

Coyotes By Night In the Wooded Hills

Out of the darkness a high pitch squeal,
        a scream.
Then silence, another feline,
pet or stray in the food chain.

These hills echo the hunt, the scene of the crime,
the lure, the ambush, the chase, the kill, the call.
They befriend their meal, a small canine friend.
Maybe lost or left out too late,
you hear the resounding betrayal.

In snarls and bites, the ambush,
the waiting true friends take their bites.
The betrayed, angry, overwhelmed with fright,
fighting for life.

The hills and all hear the struggle,
one lone pup, in the wooded hills.
It has no chance, no rescue, no escape.

Plenty a sleepless soul must be crying.
Owners of the lost,
those to whom lost ones have never returned.
The compassionate ones,
who see the unfairness in it all.

Sometimes you hear it in intervals.
The yelps are its, with an occasional howl.
The snarls are theirs with apportioned growls.
Who could find it and deliver it in these hills,
        in the middle of civilization.

They have been somewhat domesticated
in that they do wait,
until the children are asleep.

Coyotes by night in the wooded hills.

First Church

There it stands, like a beacon on a hill.
Stalwart, strong, immovable and still;
as black as black can be.

You old hospitable place, where your children's
hopes still lie in the dream of Allen.
Where your sons run free and your daughters sing
spiritual songs of New Zion.
Where your young men roar like lions
across the great divide.

First here and first in heart to call your people in.
Begin your call and let the glory bells ring.
Bring in the people from the surrounding hills.
If you only knew what you meant to us.

God's house is here, so He is happy to dwell,
with us on this fair corner,
in this rare place, some think Hell.

Man On Crutches

Why did I see him today, just now?
A man with one leg.
While I was complaining,
mulling over my sorrows,
my mistakes in life.

Why did I see him just now?
He would gladly exchange his sorrows for mine.

He hobbles along on crutches,
as if they where new to him,
as if the disaster recently occurred.
Yet he has a grin of determination,
He actually moves quite well.

I mourn his lost member.
It seems to have left him so much less.
Though I can not share his pain,
I doubt he venture raise a prayer,
were my present sorrows his.

Wisdom

Wisdom does not compete against itself,
nor does the wise against the wise.

Wise, wiser, wisest does not exist.

"Wisdom" displayed by one
does not subtract from wisdom in another.

There are the wise and there are those
who can recognize wisdom when they hear
or see it.
These should be one and the same, but they are
not.
Here is a great mystery.

Neither is wisdom in the performance of a thing,
as one may think, but rather it is in the person,
where wisdom is inextricably
a part of one's being.

Wisdom eliminates isolation,
wisdom transcends individuality,
wisdom unites,
self-capitulates
and encourages;
wisdom inspires,
arouses,
confounds
and knocks the gentle giant down.

I Do Know Things She Said

I do know things she said.
Hallowed things, unblemished by tales not dared
handed down from generation to generation.

Like the night the Great Bird descended
and covered all between its feathers,
tucked safely in the warmth of its feathers.

Like the Secret Dance of Time,
mounting, building, crescendoing to the pinnacle,
and down around the world and back into its step.

Like the Mighty Rushing Wind, caught and
swallowed whole,
and fed to men, regurgitated back again,
that it might nourish those who inherit it.

Like the Stately River Oak; planted firmly by the
shorc,
its roots winding along the riverbed, cradled,
nursing;
never weaned, suckling still, though centuries pass.

I do know things she said.

I know in which nest lies the cockatrice and where
it lays its head;
its sour brood, its poisoned prawns, with quiet
patience and resolve,
awaits the millennium gestation song.

Yes, I do know things she said.

Deep things, as deep as the ripples in the seams of
Virgo,
churning in on itself, boiling, "a million billion
suns,"
boiling, like "a pot of peas."

I do know things she said.

My Time Machine

I have a time machine in my bedroom. Many days don't work out for me. When they don't, I get into my time machine, tuck myself in, fluff the controls and advance to the future, to a new day, a new beginning, a new chance.

Sidon's Branch—Traver's Debts

Sidon 's branch is all beneath him, whispers deep and dark and clean. Traver's debts are all bequeath him, can count one without the rest. Stilled, calmed, silenced from all rebuke. Hesitantly he moves forward, towards the "Shadowy Caucus," once elevated above all; once imparted power, power to decide life and death; power to break out all encompassing. The Sword of Eden in its hand. The Great Society, the crimson scare, by the people for the people; beaten down when he sticks up, bereaved of any next of kin.

Sidon's branch is all around him, growing rich and straight and strong.
Traver's debts are still within him, while others pass without distress.
Uncrowned, unheralded, ungilded through and through. Finally he turns to heaven, reaching beyond the earth and stars; mindful of his earthly duties, conscience of his persecution; in triumph lifts his hands to pray
Many times he lost but now he rules, in heights never before known. Wonderment of wonders stark and grave, no impediment can keep him from his course, no known or conjured frill, no fears, no loss from rebuke.

Now, Sidon's branch looks down from above him, still waxing bold with earthly pride.
While, Traver's debts are now forgiven him, as now he sleeps to await the prize.

Light Air

Pristine fields of honeysuckle roll, the dogwood and black cherry in full regalia. This is where I awakened to self amid streaming flights of bumble bees, an open meadow, flowers and blossoms as far as the eye could see.

A melodious symphony, the ecstasy of life. The nature of things, of beautiful things. I searched and searched, for I knew there was one flower, that had to be touched by me and me alone in this sea of passion with a mission to touch, to seek, to find.

Fishing the Sands of Sahara

The Sahara is deep, more than a mile deep,
with shifting currents and glassy crystal,
sweeping across in dry heave waves of gritty blasts.

For additional copies of *The Soul's Sweet Simple Music* or to reach the author, please contact:

First Assist Publications
P.O. Box 608
Woodland Hills, CA 91365

Phone/Fax: (818) 700-3412

The Soul's Sweet Simple Music is $18.95 for hardbound edition, plus $4.00 shipping for first copy ($1.50 each additional copy) and sales tax for CA orders.